Congratulations to you all! May you enjoy this book for years to come!

Love, Pete + Lisa

Kibby

Gets a Little Sister

by Andrea Cassell

illustrated by Melanie Regier Koop

To:
Couto
Family
With Kibby
Kisses!
XX

Andrea Cassell

To my children and grandchildren...

WELCOME

It's a...

Kibby Gets a Little Sister

Cover design by Melanie Regier Koop
Book design and layout by Melanie Regier Koop

For more information, please contact:
Mascot Books
620 Herndon Parkway, Suite 320
Herndon, VA 20170
info@mascotbooks.com

Library of Congress Control Number: 2019917513

CPSIA Code: PRT0120A
ISBN-13: 978-1-64543-341-5

Printed in the United States

Always love one another, like I love you!

OLIVE

Little Sister

This charming story tells how Kibby reacts when he gets a new baby sister.

As a parent of four, I know all too well how challenging it can be bringing a new baby home. Sometimes it can be even more difficult for the former baby to become the older sibling. It's important to visualize and understand their confusion and feelings they may have with a new sibling.

It was a joy to write this story because it brought back warm memories of those very special days!

I hope you enjoy the story and share your memories with your children. They will learn to embrace and love each other.

With Kibby Kisses, X X
Andrea

My name is
Kibby.

I am a miniature labradoodle.

I was born on St. Patrick's Day.

Life is wonderful!

I'm a
happy dog!

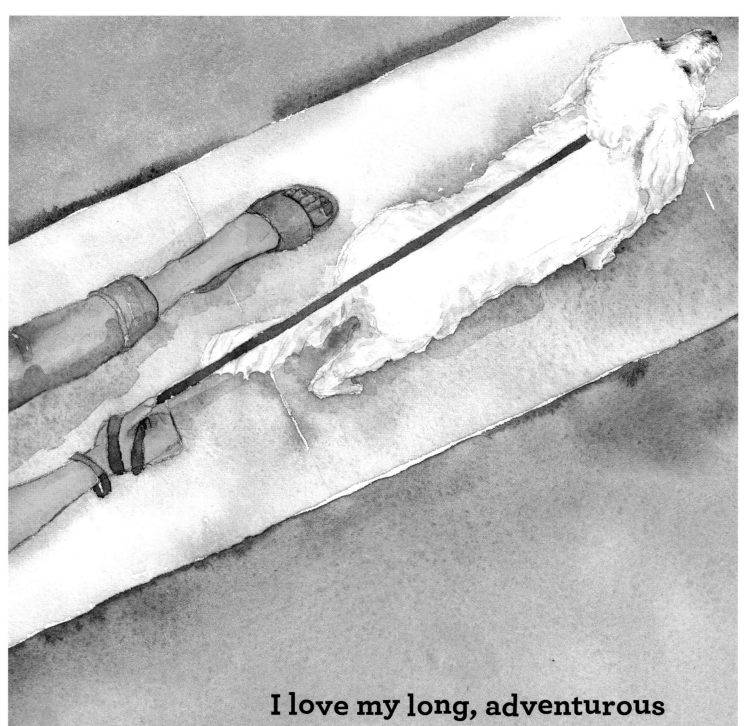

I love my long, adventurous
walks with my Mom.
She lets me lead her on my leash,
because I'm a big boy now!

Every morning, I run and get the newspaper for my Dad.

He always gives me a yummy treat.

Yum! Yum! Yum!

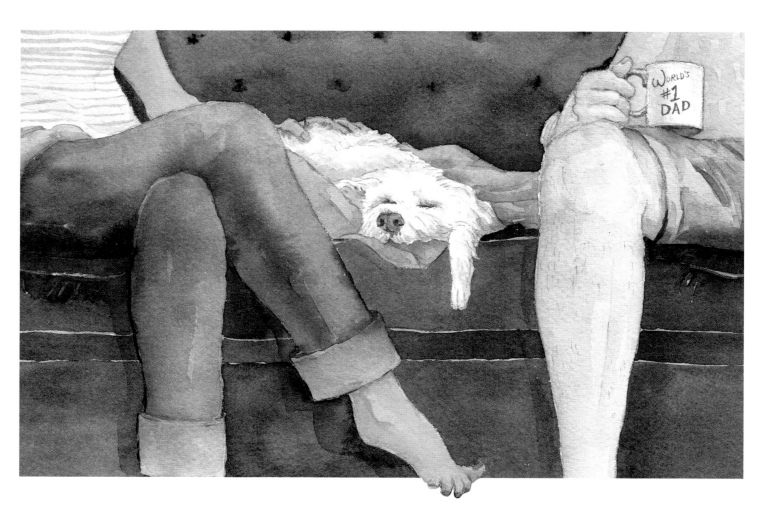

My two favorite things are snuggles and naps on the couch. I cuddle right between Mom and Dad, where it's warm and cozy.

Everyday, my Mom gives me fresh water and food. I really look forward to meal time.

I am a
happy dog!

One day, Mom came home
holding a little brown puppy.

She told me the puppy's name was Olive.
She told me Olive was going to be
my little sister.

What?!

We don't need another
dog in the house!

What's going to happen to me?

I don't think they like me anymore.

Now, my long, adventurous
walks with Mom are not the same.
She brings Olive to walk with us!

It isn't fun.
I don't get to lead.
Olive is so darn slow!

In the mornings, Dad has to take Olive outside to potty train her. He never lets me get the newspaper—he grabs it himself!

I am a sad dog!

Even snuggles and naps
are not the same.

Mom holds Olive on her lap.

When I try to jump up,

Mom says,

"You're next, Kibby. Wait your turn."

But I don't want to take turns!

Olive even drinks out of MY water bowl!

Yuck!

Yuck!

Yuck!

Olive potties on the carpet.

She tinkles everywhere!

She takes my toys
and chews on them.

Stop!

Stop!

Stop!

When I'm asleep,
she wakes me up to play.

I need my naps!

When Olive tries to kiss me,

I ignore her.

When Olive tries to play with me,

I ignore her.

I want to be the only dog in the house.

Why do Mom and Dad like her?

Things are so different since Olive moved in.

I don't get any attention from Mom and Dad.

They give it ALL to Olive!

I am a very sad dog!

So, I decide to get some attention.

I jump up on the chair.

I grab papers off the desk.

I tear them to pieces.

I take Dad's shoe and
run around the house with it.

Fun!

Fun!

Fun!

I unravel the toilet
paper from the bathroom.

But nothing I do
seems to get Mom
and Dad's attention!

I think they still love Olive more!

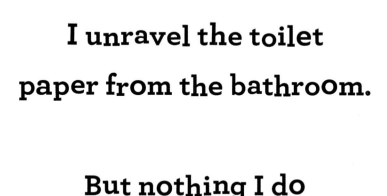

One day, Mom and Dad went out of town.
They take Olive and me to my favorite place
—Doggy Day Care.

I love Doggy Day Care!

I get to play with all kinds of dogs.

Big

and

LITTLE

dogs.

It is so much fun!

All of a sudden,

I see no one is playing with Olive.

She is sitting all alone.

She looks like a sad dog!

I feel bad for her.

I give her some kisses.

I show Olive how to play with the other dogs.

She is very nice to them and they really like her!

We all play together.

It is so much fun!

We are all happy dogs!

When we get home, Olive and I go on our
long, adventurous walks with Mom.
I show Olive how to lead Mom on the leash.

I teach Olive how to fetch the newspaper for Dad.

We both get yummy treats! Yum!

Yum!

Yum!

Olive and I take naps together on the couch.

We have our own snuggle time together.

It is so warm and cozy!

Now, I don't even mind when Olive

drinks from my water bowl!

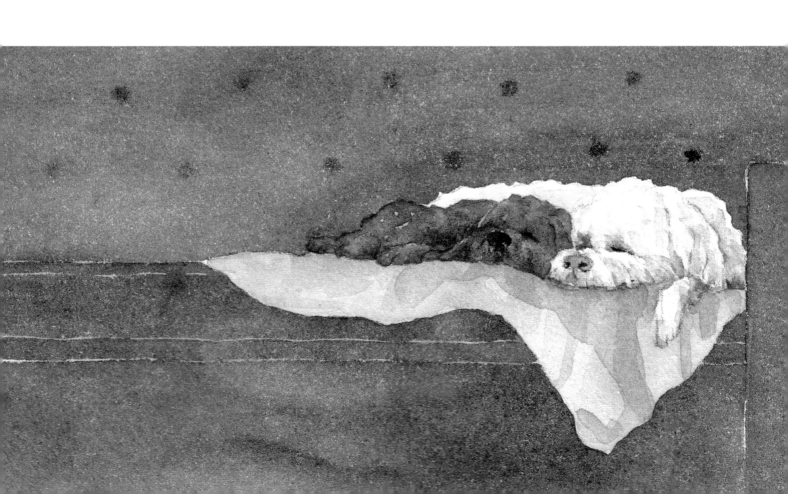

Olive learned not to potty on the carpet.

She stopped tinkling everywhere.

She learned to go outside with me.

Now, we play together.
I share my toys with her.
She gives good kisses too!

Kiss **Kiss** Kiss

I love my little sister Olive.
I am so glad I am not the
only dog in the house!

Now, I have someone to
share my walks, naps, snuggles,
toys, friends, and water with.

It is so much more fun when you
can share with a little sister!
Olive is the best!

I am a very happy dog!

I now know why Mom and Dad got Olive.
They didn't get her for them,
they got her for ME!

I am so lucky to have a little sister!

Life is wonderful!

Flip this page to see real photos of Kibby and Olive!